Classic Recipes of PERU

Classic Recipes of PERU

TRADITIONAL FOOD AND COOKING
IN 25 AUTHENTIC DISHES

FLOR ARCAYA DE DELIOT

LORENZ BOOKS

This edition is published by
Lorenz Books,
an imprint of Anness Publishing Ltd,
108 Great Russell Street,
London WC1B 3NA
info@anness.com
www.annesspublishing.com
twitter: @Anness_Books

If you like the images in this book and would like to investigate using them for publishing, promotions or advertising, please visit our website www.practicalpictures.com for more information.

Publisher: Joanna Lorenz
Editor: Helen Sudell
Designer: Nigel Partridge
Recipe Photography: Jon Whitaker
Food Stylist: Fergal Connelly
Prop Stylist: Penny Markham
Production Controller: Stephanie Moe

A CIP catalogue record for this book is available from the British Library

PUBLISHER'S NOTE

Although the advice and information in this book are believed to be accurate and true at the time of going to press, neither the authors nor the publisher can accept any legal responsibility or liability for any errors or omissions that may have been made nor for any inaccuracies nor for any loss, harm or injury that comes about from following instructions or advice in this book.

PUBLISHER'S ACKNOWLEDGMENTS

The Publisher would like to thank the following agencies for the use of their images. Istock p6, 9, 10, 11 (bottom). Alamy p11 (top).

Previously published as part of a larger volume *The Food and Cooking of Peru*.

COOK'S NOTES

Bracketed terms are intended for American readers. For all recipes, quantities are given in both metric and imperial measures and, where appropriate, in standard cups and spoons. Follow one set of measures, but not a mixture, because they are not interchangeable.

Standard spoon and cup measures are level. 1 tsp = 5ml, 1 tbsp = 15ml, 1 cup = 250ml/8fl oz. Australian standard tablespoons are 20ml. Australian readers should use 3 tsp in place of 1 tbsp for measuring small quantities.

American pints are 16fl oz/2 cups. American readers should use 20fl oz/2.5 cups in place of 1 pint when measuring liquids.

Electric oven temperatures in this book are for conventional ovens. When using a fan oven, the temperature will probably need to be reduced by about 10–20ºC/20–40ºF. Since ovens vary, you should check with your manufacturer's instruction book for guidance.

The nutritional analysis given for each recipe is calculated per portion (i.e. serving or item), unless otherwise stated. If the recipe gives a range, such as Serves 4–6, then the nutritional analysis will be for the smaller portion size, i.e. 6 servings. The analysis does not include optional ingredients, such as salt added to taste.

Medium (US large) eggs are used unless otherwise stated.

Contents

Introduction

The enchanting country of Peru covers a vast area, from the equatorial north to the temperate south, and is made up of an incredibly diverse terrain, with its long, straight Pacific coastline and snow-topped Andes mountains. Between these two extremes, Peru enjoys an amazing variety of geography and climate, which is a major factor in its culinary heritage. Traditional fare has always been based around simple meals using fresh, local ingredients, and this emphasis still holds true today.

Left: Machu Picchu, ancient home of the Incas, in the high Andes.

Peruvian Cuisine

It is said that cooks in Peru can make three meals a day for a year without precisely repeating any one of those meals, such is the variety of ingredients to be found there. It is this abundance of fresh ingredients that dictates what is eaten each day.

Mealtime routines

Some formal dining traditions from the Inca empire survived the Spanish conquest, particularly in the importance placed on special family meals, with the possible exception of breakfast. These days breakfast is often a simple matter of a milky drink and bread. At weekends families gather for a long breakfast of *tamales* and *chicharrones* served with plenty of coffee.

Below: Bread and hot chocolate is a simple breakfast meal.

Above: Rice is presented with many stews and casseroles to mop up the rich juices.

Time is put aside for the main meal of the day, usually at lunchtime, and often with friends and family. At every meal there is bread on the table plus the staple dish of rice. There will also usually be a sauce based on chilli, onion or cheese to accompany the food, and sometimes a large bowl of freshly picked salad.

Stews and casseroles are a favourite main course, especially vegetable concoctions including potatoes, corn and squash, topped with cheese. These might contain added protein in the form of pork, poultry, beef or fish. Locally grown spices such as chilli and turmeric add a kick to the simplest recipe.

When it comes to desserts and puddings, another whole area of culinary creativity opens up. Ice cream is a firm favourite, so too are the many recipes for preserving fruits in syrup. Apart from fruit-based desserts, Peruvians love to eat sponge or pastry dishes with fruit fillings, or milk-based puddings such as *suspiro a la Limena* 'the sigh of a woman from Lima', which is a delicate confection of milky custard (*manjar blanco*). There are also meringues flavoured with vanilla, or *picarones*, a sautéed dough made of squash and sweet potato drizzled with molasses and fig syrup.

Right: Corn is grown everywhere in Peru and is brightly coloured.

Food and Festivals

Over 80 per cent of Peruvians are now Catholics and the religious calendar year dictates what food is eaten and how each festival is celebrated. Underlying the Christian rituals is an older rhythm linked to the Inca tribes, whose celebrations were based on thanking and propitiating the gods of harvest, weather and the sun.

New Year

Parties to celebrate the new year are held all over the country. On 1 January, many people eat a traditional breakfast of chicacharrones (fried pork strips) and tamales (steamed corn wraps with meat or a cheese filling).

Carnival

February is carnival month in Peru. The city of Ayacucho is renowned for its elaborate celebrations, marking the period of freedom and excess before the restraints of Lent. The most famous carnival foods are chicharrones, tamales and *pachamanca* (a joint of meat – sometimes a whole carcass). These are all baked under hot stones in huge temporary ovens constructed in the street.

Above: Tamales being prepared for the New Year festivities.

Easter

The focus here is on Lenten penance and fasting until the joyous release of Easter Sunday. The special Easter dishes eaten in Peru are usually based on fish and shellfish. A favourite is Spanish-influenced *bacalao* (salted cod) mixed with chickpeas and bell peppers.

Cuzco jubilee

There are two major ceremonies in Cuzco in June, Corpus Christi – a Catholic religious ritual – and Inti Raymi, an Inca festival when the people of Cuzco honour the sun, the earth and its produce, particularly corn. The main dish is *chiri uchu* (chicken, guinea pig, corn omelette, cheese and black pudding), accompanied by *chica de jora* (a corn beverage that dates back to Inca times).

Spring festivals

The beginning of the rainy season in August is celebrated just as the Incas used to do, with the cleaning of irrigation channels and wells. Lamb stew is a favourite dish at this time. In Apurimac, the Virgin of Cocharcas is celebrated on 8th September with a procession and feasting on dishes such as *huatia* (potatoes cooked under hot stones), *japchi* (fresh cheese with spring onions, broad beans, peas and lettuce) and *picantes* (stew with garlic, onions and chilli).

The Lord of the Miracles

In October, there is a major festival in Lima: the three processions of the Lord of the Miracles. This brings together many thousands of worshippers dressed in purple. Dishes include a delicious golden sweet called *turron de Dona Pepa*, made of sugar and syrup of fig leaves. Other delights include *chicha morada*, a purple corn and fruit beverage, and *mazamorra morada*, a purple corn pudding made of the same mixture, but thickened with potato starch.

All Souls' Day

In November everyone in Peru celebrates All Souls' Day to commemorate the dead. People spend the whole night in vigil, and take flowers to the tombs of family and friends. The local cemeteries are full of visitors and in some towns the visitors bring music, food and presents for the dead, as the Incas believed that they still need sustenance in the afterlife.

Left: Male dancers at the Inti Raymi festival honour the sun, the earth and its produce.

Above: Turron de Dona Pepa, made specially for the Lord of the Miracles festival.

Christmas

The main meal of Christmas is eaten after midnight mass on Christmas Eve (now sometimes celebrated earlier, at 10pm). The Christmas menu is really lavish featuring tamales, stuffed roast turkey, salads and apple sauce, a North American introduction. During Christmas Day itself, Peruvian hot chocolate – the best in the world – and Italian panettone is served.

Classic Ingredients

In Peru it is customary for the cook of the house to shop nearly every day at the market. Meals are concocted almost entirely from what is in the store or at the market.

Meat and poultry

These days most types of meat are available in all regions of Peru. Markets carry a good range, including the popular guinea pig, once an Andean delicacy but now enjoyed all over the country fried, grilled or broiled, or roasted. Beef is another popular meat, and all parts of the animal are used; many Peruvian dishes are based on beef heart, liver, tripe and kidneys. The same is true of pork, with all parts of the pig being used. Lamb tends to be eaten mainly in the centre and south of Peru, while goat is still sometimes eaten in the north.

Chicken is a staple of Peruvian cuisine. Peruvians eat it in many guises: old tough birds were traditionally stewed to tenderize them, and then used in a range of imaginative salads.

Below: Fresh cheese has a mild flavour and soft texture.

Fish and shellfish

With its long Pacific coastline and its wide inland rivers, there are very many varieties of fish available. Two of the most popular are sea bass and lemon sole, both of which have a delicate flavour that is perfect served with a wide range of seasonings and sauces. Many of the fish eaten in Peru are not well known in other countries, but the recipes for them work well with most white fish.

Shellfish and molluscs are also found in abundance, from prawns (shrimp), crayfish, squid and octopus to scallops, mussels and whelks, all of which are transformed into delicious dishes with the addition of wonderful sauces. Many of these spiced dishes just need a plain accompaniment such as rice or potatoes to complement their piquant flavour.

Dairy produce

Peruvians love creamy food, and milk is often added to soups, stews, puddings and drinks. Canned condensed milk is often used instead of fresh. A good range of cheese is made in the different regions of Peru according to local customs and the kind of milk available – from cows, sheep or goats. Fresh cheese, sprinkled with salt, is a young, soft white cheese typical of the central Mantaro region. The cheese from the northern mountains has a creamy, buttery texture that melts easily when heated.

Right: Seafood, such as these richly coloured clams, is popular along the Pacific coastline.

Above: Dried green peas are used in many stews.

Pulses, grains and nuts

Dried beans, lentils and cereals are a basic, cheap, nourishing food found in many homes. Butter (lima) beans, green and red lentils, chickpeas, dried green peas, quinoa, and the very Peruvian 'canario' (canary beans) with their yellowish colour and unique taste, are all widely available. Grains such as corn, rice and wheat also form a major part of the diet, whether used whole in stews and soups for bulk or ground into flour to make bread.

Corn on the cob is grown everywhere in Peru and is also eaten in many different ways, whether as a main ingredient or on its own with butter, as well as forming the basis of chicha, the Peruvians' national drink.

Vegetables

Potatoes are one of the basic ingredients of Peruvian cooking. There are many varieties of potato, each with its own unique characteristics. Yellow potatoes are floury and tend to crumble; these are best suited to spicy marinades with chilli. White potatoes are firmer and cook well in stews and soups without falling apart. 'Huayro' potatoes are softer, with a hint of sweetness.

After the staple potato, tomatoes are the most popular vegetable in Peru. They are served hot or cold, cooked or raw and made into sauces and marinades. All sizes are for sale, from tasty plum tomatoes right up to the giant beefsteak varieties. Onions and garlic feature in marinades, and are the basis of many stews as they bring out the flavour of other ingredients.

Above: Potatoes feature in many Peruvian meals.

There are many kinds of green leaves sold as salad vegetables or for cooking, for example a wide variety of lettuces, spinach and kale. These leaves complement the sturdier vegetables such as cucumber, squash and sweet bell peppers.

Peruvian recipes use all kinds of squash including small and large courgettes (zucchini), medium-sized butternut squash and pumpkins, which can grow to an enormous size. Sweet potatoes are a versatile vegetable that blends with both sweet and savoury flavours, giving a lift to both.

Cassava and plantain are favourites of the people of the rainforest, and grow well there in the steamy heat.

Fruit

Like the vegetable stalls, fruit stalls are full of different colours and aromas. The important principle when buying fruit is very simple: any fruit that does not have a strong smell is not ripe; any fruit that does not have a strong colour is not sweet. Any Peruvian coming to a fruit counter will want to sniff the peaches, papayas, melons, pineapples, apples, mangoes and plums. The few fruits that do not give off a sweet smell because of their thick skins, such as passion fruit and watermelons, can be selected by feel – they should feel heavy – and sometimes by colour.

Below: Mangoes are a colourful fruit favoured by Peruvians.

As well as the fruits available in most parts of the world, Peru has species of fruit unknown elsewhere, such as camu camu, lucuma, cocona and aguaje.

Herbs and spices

Although many herbs and spices are used in Peruvian recipes, the most important is undoubtedly the chilli pepper. The first chillies were native to the Andes, and eaten by the men and women who lived there thousands of years ago. In Peru, the chilli is almost a sacred ingredient, symbolizing wealth and strength. Even now, men will encourage each other to add chilli to their food as a test of their virility.

Spice counters in the markets sell some ingredients ready prepared, such as peeled garlic, chilli sauces and dressings both fresh and dried, cinnamon, salt, turmeric, cumin, saffron and ginger. Many of these are known to have been consumed by the Incas; others were imported by African or Chinese cooks.

Above: Turmeric adds a lovely earthy flavour to casseroles.

The herbs used in Peru are a good mixture of indigenous varieties, especially all kinds of mint, and those brought by the Spanish in the 16th century. The fresh leaves of coriander (cilantro), and the various flavours of parsley, basil, saffron and rosemary enhance many dishes, and are used in dressings and marinades alongside the stronger onion and garlic.

Flavours of Peru

To the untrained eye, Peruvian recipes can appear simple and repetitive, especially when so many feature potatoes and corn. However, to Peruvian tastebuds, there is a world of difference between one subtly flavoured dish and another. Peruvian cuisine relies on cooking basic recipes with an almost infinite number of creative variations according to what is available in the market. From spicy Cebiche and fruit-filled Empanaditas to Squash, Potato and Corn Stew and Cassavas stuffed with Cheese, this collection of authentic recipes offer a wealth of tastes and flavours.

Left: Peruvians love soup, whether a simple bowl of consommé or a hearty bowl of several ingredients, such as this colourful crayfish soup (see page 30).

Serves 8

1kg/2¼lb pork belly, cut into 2.5cm/1in squares
5ml/1 tsp salt
1 litre/1¾ pints/4 cups water
fried sliced sweet potatoes (see cook's tip), to serve

For the onion salsa:

1 red onion, sliced
juice of 1 lime
30ml/2 tbsp vegetable oil
1 chilli, seeded and thinly sliced
salt

Fried Pork with Onion Salsa
Chicharrones

1 Put the pork in a large pan and add the salt and just enough water to cover the meat. Bring to the boil and leave to simmer, uncovered, until all the water has evaporated.

2 Meanwhile, make the onion salsa. Put the sliced onion in a dish and sprinkle with 15ml/1 tbsp salt. Place a plate on top and weight it down with something heavy. Leave for 10–15 minutes until the onion has released its juices, then rinse off the salt and drain thoroughly, squeezing out the liquid. Repeat, then add the lime juice, oil, sliced chilli and a pinch of salt.

3 Once the water has boiled off the pork, continue to cook the meat gently so that it fries in its own fat. Turn the pieces until they are golden on all sides. Serve the chicharrones accompanied by the onion salsa and fried sliced sweet potatoes.

COOK'S TIP

To make fried sweet potatoes, thickly slice four large sweet potatoes and drop into a large pan of boiing water, turn the heat down and simmer for 5 minutes. Add 30ml/2 tbsp vegetable oil to a large, heavy frying pan and fry gently for about 10 minutes, turning occasionally, until they are cooked through and golden in colour.

This is one of the most famous of all Peruvian dishes. Food stores and stalls cook it in huge pans called pailas, which will hold a whole quarter of pork cut into pieces. For breakfast it's eaten in a sandwich with fried sliced sweet potato and onion salsa; at lunchtime it is often served on a plate accompanied by boiled cassava.

Marinated Fish Cebiche

Serves 4

500g/1¼lb firm white fish fillets such as cod, halibut or coley, skinless and boneless
½ medium red onion, sliced lengthways
1 chilli, seeded and sliced
2 celery sticks, thinly sliced
juice of 8 limes, about 150ml/10 tbsp
4–8 lettuce leaves, to garnish
15ml/1 tbsp finely chopped parsley, to garnish
salt and ground black pepper

To accompany:

2 medium sweet potatoes, peeled and cut into chunks
500g/1¼lb cassava, peeled and cut into chunks
1 corn on the cob

1 Cut the fish into bitesize pieces about 2cm/¾in across, and place in a bowl with the onion, chilli and celery. Season well with salt and pepper.

2 Pour the lime juice over the mixture and stir gently to distribute it evenly. Cover and leave to marinate for 15 minutes, then stir again and leave for another 15 minutes. The fish is ready when it has become opaque.

3 Meanwhile, boil the sweet potatoes in unsalted water for 25 minutes and boil the cassava in salted water for 20 minutes, until tender. Cut the corn on the cob into four pieces and boil in unsalted water for 10–15 minutes.

4 Arrange the lettuce leaves around the edge of a serving dish and pile the fish mixture in the middle. Garnish with parsley and serve immediately, accompanied by sweet potatoes, corn on the cob and cassava.

COOK'S TIP

To serve cebiche as a snack to accompany drinks, cut the fish into smaller pieces and arrange spoonfuls of the mixture in small scallop shells. You may prefer to marinate the fish for more or less time: experiment with the timing to see how you like it best.

This dish is mentioned in Peruvian literature from the 19th century, and its roots are much older. The raw fish is 'cooked' by the action of citrus juice, originally from sour oranges, which once grew abundantly on the coast. Cebiche, or ceviche, is now eaten all along the Pacific coast, and every country has its own version.

Potatoes in Peanut Sauce
Papas con mani

Serves 6

500g/1¼lb white potatoes
75ml/5 tbsp vegetable oil
250g/9oz red onion, finely chopped
30ml/2 tbsp green chilli sauce (see cook's tip)
250g/9oz/2 cups shelled peanuts, ground
salt
3 hard-boiled eggs, quartered, lettuce leaves, and sections of cooked corn (optional) to serve

1 Boil the potatoes in lightly salted water for about 25 minutes, until tender. Remove from the heat, drain and peel. Keep them warm.

2 Heat the oil in a frying pan and fry the onion for about 10 minutes until it starts to caramelize. Add the chilli sauce and the peanuts and cook for 2–3 minutes, stirring. Remove from the heat.

3 Lay one or two lettuce leaves on each plate. Slice the potatoes and pile them in the centre. Pour the sauce over the potatoes and add two quarters of egg, and sections of corn if using.

COOK'S TIP

For green chilli sauce, remove the pith and seeds from 6 green chillies. Fry in oil with ½ chopped red onion and 2 chopped garlic cloves until the onion is soft. Add salt to taste. Remove from the heat and purée in a blender or food processor.

Peanuts have been eaten in Peru for many centuries, and are depicted in jewellery and other artefacts made by pre-Inca cultures. They are often used to make sauces for traditional Inca meats such as guinea pig, rabbit or pigs' feet, but in this recipe they partner potatoes. The dish is served warm.

Broad Bean and Fresh Cheese Salad
Solterito de habas

Serves 4

250g/9oz small white potatoes
250g/9oz/2 cups shelled broad (fava) beans
kernels of 1 fresh corn on the cob or 1 medium can corn in unsalted water
150g/5oz feta cheese, cut into 1cm/½in dice
15ml/1 tbsp white wine vinegar
45ml/3 tbsp olive oil
1 fresh red or green chilli, seeded and finely chopped
salt and ground black pepper

Broad beans are very dear to the Peruvian people. They are used in soups, stews and many other dishes, and, when young and freshly picked, are eaten raw as a snack. This is a substantial salad that makes a satisfying first course.

1 Boil the potatoes in lightly salted water for 20 minutes, until tender. Drain and allow to cool for 10 minutes, then gently slide the skin off with your fingers and cut into 1cm/½in dice.

2 Boil the broad beans in lightly salted water for 15 minutes. Drain and allow to cool, then pop them out of their skins. If the beans are young and small you need not do this.

3 If using fresh corn on the cob, boil for 10 minutes, then drain and slice off the kernels with a sharp knife. Leave to cool. If using canned corn, drain it.

4 Mix the potatoes, beans and corn kernels with the cheese in a salad bowl and dress with the vinegar, oil, salt and pepper. Sprinkle the chilli on top and serve.

Peruvian Beef Pies Empanaditas

Makes 20 small pies

For the filling:

75ml/5 tbsp vegetable oil
450g/1lb/2 cups minced (ground) beef
1 large red onion, finely chopped
150g/5oz/1 cup raisins, chopped
150g/5oz/1 cup kalamata olives, pitted and chopped
250ml/8fl oz/1 cup water
3 hard-boiled eggs, diced
salt

For the pastry:

450g/1lb self-raising (self-rising) flour
1.5ml/¼ tsp salt
150g/5oz margarine
60ml/4 tbsp water
150g/5oz/1¼ cups icing (confectioners') sugar

1 To make the filling, heat the oil in a large frying pan and fry the minced beef for 5–10 minutes, stirring, until browned. Stir in the onion and fry until it is starting to caramelize, then add the raisins and olives.

2 Add the water to the pan and season to taste with salt. Cover and simmer for 10 minutes, then remove from the heat and leave to cool while you make the pastry.

3 Sift the flour into a large mixing bowl and add the salt. Rub in the margarine with your fingers. Add the water and knead until the dough is smooth and not sticky. Cover the bowl with a clean dish towel or clear film (plastic wrap) and leave it to rest for 15 minutes. Preheat the oven to 200°C/400°F/Gas 6.

4 Roll out the dough thinly on a floured surface and cut out 6cm/2½in circles using a cookie cutter. Spoon a little of the cooled filling (avoiding any liquid) on to each circle and add a piece of hard-boiled egg.

5 Fold the dough circle in half over the stuffing, wet the rim with a little water and pinch the edges together with your fingers. Place on an oiled baking tray, well spaced so the pies have room to spread. Bake for 15 minutes or until they are golden.

6 Leave the pastries on the tray to cool. Dust with sifted icing sugar before serving. Eat with the fingers.

Empanaditas have been part of Peru's culinary history since the first days of Spanish rule. The little pies filled with beef, chicken or cheese make very popular mid-morning snacks and are sold in bakeries and from street stalls all over the country. These miniature versions make wonderful party appetizers.

Corn Parcels Humitas

Makes 8 parcels

6 fresh corn cobs, with husks
125g/4¼oz lard
15ml/1 tbsp garlic purée
15ml/1 tbsp chilli sauce
15ml/1 tbsp mild chilli sauce
250g/9oz/1 cup cornmeal or fine polenta
salt
onion salsa, to serve (see page 18)

For the filling:

45ml/3 tbsp vegetable oil
1 small red onion, thickly sliced lengthways
1 small chilli, seeded and thinly sliced lengthways
2.5ml/½ tsp salt
½ cooked chicken breast fillet, shredded
2 hard-boiled eggs, quartered

Corn or maize has been cultivated for more than 7,000 years in the Americas and it is still a staple food, especially in Central America and Mexico.

1 Remove the husks from the corn cobs (see cook's tip) and boil the leaves in water for 10 minutes to soften, drain and cover.

2 Heat the oil for the filling in a frying pan and fry the onion and chilli until softened. Remove from the heat, add the salt and set aside.

3 Slice the kernels from the corn cobs (reserving the cobs) and blend the kernels to a paste in a blender or food processor.

4 Melt the lard in a large pan, and fry the garlic purée. Add the two chilli sauces, the corn paste, the cornmeal or polenta, and a pinch of salt.

5 Reduce the heat and cook the mixture for 10–15 minutes or until it forms a thick dough, stirring constantly to stop it sticking to the pan. When it is very thick, remove from the heat.

6 To prepare each parcel, spread out a piece of corn husk then lay a second piece over it, with the wide ends overlapping.

7 Spoon 30ml/2 tbsp of the corn mixture into the centre of the leaves. Add a piece of chicken, some fried onion and a piece of hard-boiled egg. Cover with another 30ml/2 tbsp of corn. Fold in the sides of the leaves, then the ends, to form a parcel. Tie loosely with string as the filling will expand during cooking. Repeat to make seven more parcels.

8 Place the reserved corn cobs in the bottom of a large pan and pour in just enough water to cover them. Lay any remaining pieces of husk over the cobs and place the parcels on top, so they will cook in the steam. Bring to the boil and cook, covered, over a low heat for 1 hour. Remove the parcels and leave to cool for a while before opening them carefully. Serve accompanied by onion salsa.

COOK'S TIP

Before stripping the leaves, cut around each cob about 2.5cm/1in from the bottom. Do the same at the top, then remove all the leaves, discarding the outer ones but collecting the rest for wrapping the parcels.

Butter Bean Soup Sopa de pallares

Serves 6

250g/9oz/1¼ cups butter (lima) beans, soaked overnight in plenty of water
2 large white potatoes, peeled and quartered
2 beef stock (bouillon) cubes
75ml/5 tbsp vegetable oil
1 medium red onion, finely chopped
1 garlic clove, finely chopped
2.5ml/½ tsp paprika
2.5ml/½ tsp dried oregano
250ml/8fl oz/1 cup full cream (whole) milk
45ml/3 tbsp hard, strong cheese, such as Parmesan, grated, to serve
salt

1 Wash and drain the butter beans and put them in a large pan with 2 litres/3½ pints/8 cups fresh water. Bring to the boil, cover and simmer for 1 hour, until tender.

2 Meanwhile, put the potatoes in a large pan with 1 litre/1¾ pints/4 cups water and the stock cubes. Bring to the boil, cover and simmer for 15 minutes, until tender. Remove from the heat and set aside.

3 Heat the oil in a frying pan over medium heat and fry the onion with the garlic for 10 minutes, adding the paprika and oregano when they begin to caramelize. Add this mixture to the pan of potatoes and stock, then add the beans and their cooking water.

4 Bring the soup to the boil, reduce the heat and simmer for 5 minutes. Add the milk, season to taste and serve with grated cheese.

Pulses are a staple food in Peru, and most people eat them at least once a week. Butter (lima) beans are grown in the south and are much appreciated. Like most Peruvian recipes, this one concentrates on a main ingredient, with other spices to enhance, not disguise or overwhelm, its natural flavour.

Crayfish Soup
Chupe de camarones

1 If the crayfish are living, bring a large pan of water to the boil. Add the crayfish or prawns to the water and boil for 3–5 minutes until they change colour. Remove from the pan, reserving the stock, dry with kitchen paper, devein them, and set aside.

2 Heat the oil in a large pan over high heat and add the tomato. Cook for 2 minutes, stirring, then add 1 litre/1¾ pints/4 cups of crayfish stock, or water.

3 Add the potato, butternut squash, beans, rice, corn and salt to the pan. Bring to the boil, then lower the heat and simmer for 15 minutes, until the potatoes are almost cooked.

4 Break the eggs into the hot soup, taking care that each one stays separate from the others. Simmer for 10–15 minutes, then remove from the heat. Stir in the milk and serve, distributing the crayfish evenly and adding a poached egg to each bowl.

Serves 6

1kg/2¼lb fresh crayfish or king prawns (jumbo shrimp)
75ml/5 tbsp vegetable oil
1 large tomato, diced
1 litre/1¾ pints/4 cups cooking stock or water
6 medium floury potatoes, peeled and cut into chunks
250g/9oz butternut squash, cut into cubes
250g/9oz/1½ cups shelled and skinned broad (fava) beans
100g/3¾oz/½ cup long grain rice
2 corn cobs, cut into chunks
7.5ml/1½ tsp salt
6 eggs
350ml/12fl oz evaporated milk

This is one of the most special of all Peruvian dishes. The word chupe can be translated as 'chowder', and it means a hearty soup containing meat or fish, eggs, potatoes, vegetables and rice or noodles; a complete meal in one dish. In many parts of the world fishmongers sell crayfish live, in which case they are quickly immersed in boiling water, before being cleaned.

Beef Hotpot Sancochado

Serves 4

1kg/2¼lb beef brisket
4 litres/7 pints/17½ cups water
1 large celery heart
1 small Savoy cabbage, halved
500g/1¼lb potatoes, peeled
500g/1¼lb carrots, peeled
500g/1¼lb cassava, peeled
2 corn on the cob
500g/1¼lb sweet potatoes, peeled
salt

Sancochado is regarded as a national dish, though there are some regional variations. It developed from a Spanish dish, cocido, a substantial soup made from meats and vegetables, and is often accompanied by onion and chilli salsa.

1 Put the beef into a large pan with the water and add 15ml/1 tbsp salt, the celery heart and the cabbage. Bring to the boil, reduce the heat, skim and simmer, covered, for 45 minutes.

2 Roughly chop the potatoes, carrots, cassava and corn and add to the pan. Cook for 20 minutes. When the root vegetables are tender, lift them out together with the celery and cabbage and keep warm.

3 Add the sweet potatoes to the soup and continue to simmer gently. When the meat and the sweet potatoes are tender, lift them out and arrange them on the serving dish with the other vegetables.

4 Serve the broth in bowls, either adding the meat and vegetables to each bowl, or serving them separately with onion and chilli salsa.

COOK'S TIP

While the soup is cooking keep checking that it does not reduce too much and add more water if necessary: you should finish up with about 2 litres/3½ pints/8 cups of soup. Try to keep the vegetables intact, draining them carefully when they are done.

Corn Purée with Fried Fish
Espesado norteno con pescado frito

Serves 4

4 fresh corn cobs
500ml/17fl oz/generous 2 cups water
25g/1oz fresh coriander (cilantro)
150ml/5fl oz/⅔ cup vegetable oil
1 medium red onion, finely chopped
2 chicken or vegetable stock (bouillon) cubes
1.5ml/¼ tsp ground cumin
10ml/2 tsp chilli sauce
4 fish fillets, such as mahi mahi or halibut
40g/1½oz plain (all-purpose) flour
salt and ground black pepper
lime halves, to serve

1 Slice the kernels off the corn cobs and blend them with half the water in a blender or food processor. Transfer to a bowl and set aside.

2 Put the coriander in the blender with half the remaining water, and blend to a purée.

3 Heat 30ml/2 tbsp of the oil in a deep pan and fry the onion until golden. Add the stock cubes, cumin, chilli sauce and the remaining water. Stir until the stock cubes have dissolved.

4 Add the blended corn kernels and simmer for 5–10 minutes, stirring constantly to avoid the mixture sticking. Stir in the coriander purée and cook for 1 minute, then remove from the heat. Pour into a serving dish and keep warm.

5 Season the fish fillets with salt and pepper and dust them with a little flour. Fry them in the remaining oil, turning once, until golden on both sides and cooked through. Serve immediately with the corn purée and half a lime.

Peruvian corn was developed in the age of the Incas, or maybe even earlier. There are two basic kinds: one from the coast, which has a large white kernel with a bland flavour, and one from the mountains, which is sweeter and crisper. This recipe can be made with the kind of fresh corn on the cob that is available everywhere.

Dry Fish Stew with Coriander
Seco de pescado

Serves 6

6 white fish fillets, such as cod or swordfish
1 large red onion, sliced lengthways
1 red (bell) pepper, thinly sliced
3 garlic cloves
2.5cm/1in piece fresh root ginger
100g/3¾oz fresh coriander (cilantro)
1.5ml/¼ tsp ground cumin
45ml/3 tbsp chilli sauce
120ml/4fl oz/½ cup vegetable oil
120ml/4fl oz/½ cup white beer
250g/9oz/2 cups shelled peas
juice of 1 lime
salt and ground black pepper
boiled rice, to serve

A seco is a 'dry' style of stew that can be made with fish or meat. This recipe, from northern Peru, uses coriander and other locally grown ingredients. Northern cooking includes many versions of seco made with chicken, kid and lamb.

1 Arrange the fish fillets in a wide pan and cover with the slices of onion and red pepper.

2 Put the garlic, ginger, coriander, cumin, chilli sauce and oil into a blender or food processor and blend to a purée. Spoon over the fish and leave to marinate for 15 minutes.

3 Put the pan on a high heat until the fish is starting to sizzle, pour in the beer and add the peas and bring to the boil. Reduce the heat, cover the pan and simmer for 15 minutes.

4 When the fish is cooked, squeeze the lime juice over the top, and serve with rice.

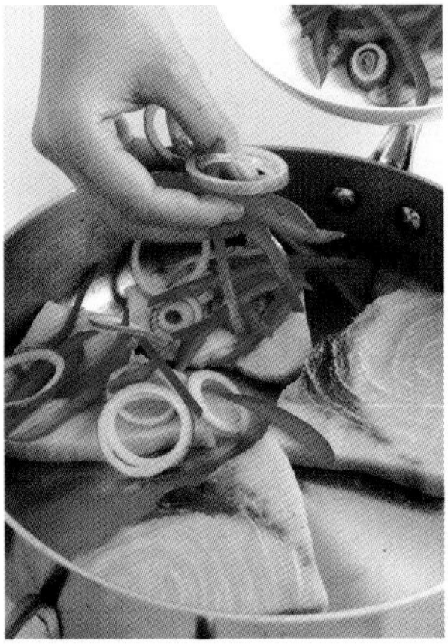

Fried Seafood Platter Jalea de mariscos

Serves 4

12 mussels, fresh or frozen
12 small squid
12 clams
6 scallops
12 raw king prawn (jumbo shrimp) tails
500g/1¼lb cassava, cut into chunks
2 medium red onions, finely sliced lengthways
juice of 2 limes
1 fresh chilli, sliced
30ml/2 tbsp chopped parsley
250ml/8fl oz/1 cup vegetable oil
500g/1¼lb firm-fleshed white fish, such as mahi mahi, cut into 2.5cm/1in chunks
250g/9oz/2 cups cornflour (cornstarch)
salt and ground black pepper

1 If using fresh mussels, scrub and remove the beard. Clean and slice the squid. Steam open the clams and scallops in a little boiling water, and remove the meat from the shells. Discard any shells that remain open when tapped. Cut the dark part of the mussel away if you wish. Peel the king prawn tails.

2 Boil the cassava for 20 minutes in lightly salted water, then drain and dry with a clean dishtowel. Season with salt and pepper.

3 Mix the sliced onions with the lime juice, chilli and parsley and set aside.

4 Heat some of the oil in a large frying pan and fry the pieces of cassava until they are golden on all sides. Transfer them to a serving dish or platter and keep warm.

5 Season the pieces of fish and dust with cornflour. Fry the fish in the remaining oil over medium-high heat for 2–3 minutes, turning, until it is an even golden brown colour. Remove from the pan with a slotted spoon and drain thoroughly on kitchen paper, then arrange over the fried cassava and keep warm.

6 Repeat with each type of seafood, frying it in batches over a high heat so that it cooks quickly without becoming tough. Remove each batch and drain on kitchen paper, then arrange on the dish with the fish.

7 When all the seafood is prepared, sprinkle the onions and lime juice on top. Place the dish on the table for everyone to help themselves.

Peruvians are very keen on dishes of bitesize, crispy fried morsels. This dish is normally accompanied by fried cassava and onion salsa, and is served on a single dish or platter for everyone to help themselves.

Beef Stew with Carrots and Potatoes
Estofado de carne

Serves 4

500g/1¼lb rump (round) steak
90ml/6 tbsp vegetable oil
1 large onion, diced
1 large tomato, chopped
500g/1¼lb potatoes, peeled and halved
250g/9oz carrots, peeled and cut in batons
250g/9oz/2 cups shelled peas
250ml/8fl oz/1 cup passata (bottled strained tomatoes)
2 bay leaves
1 litre/1¾ pints/4 cups water
salt

1 Cut the beef into 4cm/1½in cubes. Heat the oil in a large pan and fry the beef quickly, turning, until browned on all sides. Remove the beef from the pan and set aside.

2 Reduce the heat to medium-high. Add the onion and fry until golden. Return the beef to the pan and add the chopped tomato.

3 Add the remaining ingredients and season with salt. Bring to the boil, cover and simmer for 30 minutes, or until the meat is tender. Serve.

COOK'S TIP

If you use a cheaper cut of beef, such as braising (stewing) steak, increase the cooking time to 1 hour. This stew can also be made using chicken instead of beef.

This casserole is similar to many found throughout the world, but also very Peruvian. Many Peruvians consider it to be especially characteristic of Cuzco, but the dish actually has its roots in several Peruvian cities, especially those that had a substantial Spanish population after the conquest. Almost as soon as the Spanish began to cook with tomatoes, this combination of ingredients was developed. Estofado is usually served with plain rice.

Lamb Stew with Cassava
Seco de cordero

Serves 4

500g/1¼lb boneless lamb leg steaks
90ml/6 tbsp vegetable oil
1 medium onion, finely chopped
5ml/1 tsp ground cumin
15ml/1 tbsp chilli sauce
1 bunch coriander (cilantro)
1 litre/1¾ pints/4 cups water
500g/1¼lb white potatoes, peeled and halved
500g/1¼lb cassava, peeled and cut into 7.5cm/3in chunks
250g/9oz/2 cups shelled peas
salt
boiled white rice and green chilli sauce, to serve

1 Cut the meat into 5cm/2in pieces. Heat the oil in a large pan and fry the meat over medium to high heat until browned on all sides. Reduce the heat, add the onion and fry until it is golden, then add the cumin and chilli sauce.

2 Purée the coriander in a blender or processor with 250ml/8fl oz/1 cup of the water.

3 Add the coriander paste to the pan with the remaining water and bring to the boil, then add the potatoes, cassava and peas. Season.

4 Cover the pan and leave to simmer for 30 minutes, or until the meat and vegetables are tender. Serve immediately with white rice and chilli sauce.

Stews are very much part of the Peruvian kitchen, as home cooks enjoy following recipes and appreciate a clever combination of ingredients. This kind of stew, called seco (dry) to distinguish it from the soupy aguadito, contains potatoes, cassava, coriander, chilli and spices. It is served with rice and often with beans too, and with green chilli sauce on the table for those who like extra heat.

Rabbit in Peanut Sauce Conejo en salsa de mani

Serves 4
4 rabbit leg joints
250ml/8fl oz/1 cup red wine vinegar
2 rosemary sprigs
10ml/2 tsp ground paprika
4 garlic cloves, crushed
2.5ml/½ tsp ground black pepper
60ml/4 tbsp vegetable oil
250ml/8fl oz/1 cup white wine
250ml/8fl oz/1 cup water
1 quince or large cooking apple, peeled and sliced
200g/7oz/1¾ cups roasted, salted peanuts, ground in a blender
salt

There were wild rabbits in the Americas before the Spanish arrived, but that population was added to by escaped rabbits brought as food. A good way to enjoy rabbit is deep-fried (chicharrones de conejo), but it is normally eaten roasted, or in stews like this one. Serve it with white rice and boiled cassava.

1 Put the rabbit joints in a bowl with the vinegar, rosemary, paprika, garlic, black pepper and salt and leave to marinate for 2 hours.

2 Heat the oil over high heat. Dry the pieces of rabbit and fry on each side, until browned.

3 Add the wine and the water to the pan together with the slices of quince or apple and the peanuts. Bring to the boil then reduce the heat to medium, cover the pan and simmer for 30 minutes, until the rabbit is tender.

Turkey and Corn Stew Pepian de pavo

Serves 4

6 corn cobs
90ml/6 tbsp vegetable oil
500g/1¼lb skinless turkey breast fillet, cut into 2cm/¾in cubes
1 medium onion, finely chopped
2 garlic cloves, sliced or crushed
2 red chillies, seeded, blended to a purée in 60ml/4 tbsp water
500ml/17fl oz/generous 2 cups chicken stock
salt
chopped parsley, to garnish
boiled white rice, to serve

Turkey is a very popular meat in the north of Peru. The cooking techniques vary depending on the age at which the turkeys are killed. Normally a dish like this, which quickly fries the meat, would be prepared with the tender breast meat from a young female bird.

1 Using a sharp knife, strip the kernels from the corn on the cob. Put them in batches in a blender or food processor and blend to a paste.

2 Heat the oil in a large pan and fry the turkey over a high heat for 8–10 minutes, until golden on all sides. Stir in the onion and garlic, reduce the heat slightly and cook until the onion is caramelized.

3 Add the chilli purée and cook for 3 minutes, then pour in the chicken stock. Bring to the boil and allow to simmer for 20 minutes. Season to taste with salt.

4 Add the puréed corn and simmer for a further 15 minutes, until thick. Garnish with parsley and serve the turkey stew with boiled white rice.

Duck with Rice Arroz con pato

Serves 4

1kg/2¼lb duck leg joints
large bunch fresh coriander (cilantro)
vegetable oil, for frying
1 medium onion, finely chopped
2 garlic cloves, crushed or sliced
2 medium red (bell) peppers, sliced
5ml/1 tsp ground cumin
1 whole yellow chilli (see cook's tip)
60ml/4 tbsp pisco or 500ml/
17fl oz/generous 2 cups beer
250g/9oz/2 cups shelled peas
500g/1¼lb American long grain rice
salt

1 Pierce the skin of the duck all over with a fork, wash and dry with kitchen paper.

2 Put the coriander leaves in a blender or food processor with 500ml/17fl oz/generous 2 cups water and blend to a purée.

3 Heat a little oil in a large pan and, when very hot, fry the duck pieces, moving them around until browned on all sides. Remove from the pan and set aside on a plate.

4 Reduce the heat to medium, add the onion and garlic to the pan and fry until softened and golden brown.

5 Return the duck to the pan with the coriander purée and sliced peppers. Season with salt and cumin and pour in 500ml/17fl oz/generous 2 cups water.

6 Increase the heat and bring to the boil, place the whole yellow chilli on top, reduce the heat and simmer, covered, for 20 minutes.

7 When the duck is cooked, add the pisco or beer, peas and rice. Keep the heat at medium-high for 15 minutes, until the rice is partially cooked, then remove and reserve the whole chilli. Reduce the heat, stir the rice gently and simmer on a low heat, covered, for a further 10 minutes until the liquid is absorbed.

8 Serve immediately, dividing the duck portions among the diners and offering the cooked chilli to those who want extra heat.

This classic recipe for duck with rice comes from the north coast, especially the regions of La Libertad, Lambayeque and Piura. The best accompaniment is a very cold beer, though Peruvians also drink chicha de jora with this.

COOK'S TIP

The yellow chilli is a Peruvian speciality. If you cannot find it, you can add a mild chilli (such as a large red one), keeping it intact. If it is cut up it will make the whole dish hot, but if kept whole it will release flavour rather than heat.

Cassava Stuffed with Cheese
Yucas rellenas con queso

Serves 6

1.5kg/3¼lb cassava
1 egg
100g/3¾oz plain (all-purpose) flour
200g/7oz mild-flavoured, buttery cheese, such as Cheddar, or Edam, cut into 12 small pieces
250ml/8fl oz/1 cup vegetable oil
salt
boiled rice and onion or chilli salsa, to serve

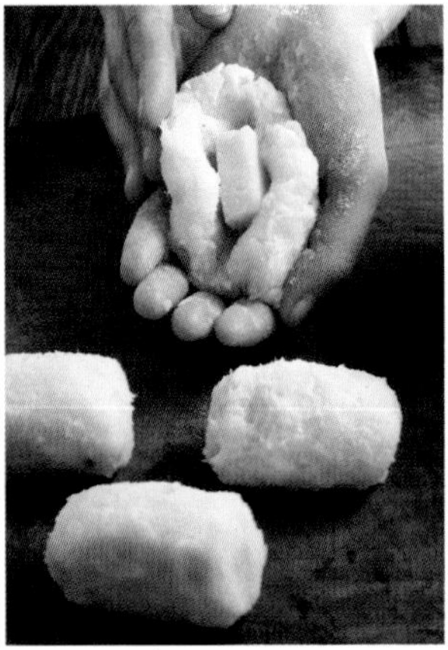

1 Cut the ends off the cassava and chop it into 7.5cm/3in sections. Remove the peel by making a lengthways cut and opening the skin with a knife. Place the peeled cassava in a large pan with water to cover and 5ml/1 tsp salt. Bring to the boil and simmer, covered, for 25 minutes.

2 When the cassava is tender, drain it and mash it while still warm. Beat in the egg and season with 5ml/1 tsp salt. Spread the mash on to a tray or board to cool.

3 Cover your palm lightly in flour, spread some of the cassava mash on to your palm, place a piece of cheese in the centre and close the mixture around it, sealing it well, to make an oval-shaped ball. Roll the ball in flour and place on a plate. Repeat to make 12 balls.

4 Heat the oil in a pan and fry the balls over high heat until golden, turning them carefully to avoid breaking. Don't crowd the pan: it is best to fry two at a time. Drain on kitchen paper and serve with rice and onion or chilli salsa.

Cassava originates from tropical America. It is said that the Maya first grew this tuberous plant for food, but it is much used by all the Amazonian tribes, who even brew an alcoholic beverage from it, called masato. There are around 160 varieties, adapted to different growing conditions. Cassava has been eaten in Peru for a long time, usually as an accompaniment but also in tasty recipes like this one.

Quinoa Stew Pesque de quinua

Serves 4

250g/9oz/1½ cups quinoa, well washed in at least 3 changes of water
1 litre/1¾ pints/4 cups water
250ml/8fl oz/1 cup fresh full cream (whole) milk or evaporated milk
60ml/4 tbsp vegetable oil
2 eggs, beaten
250g/9oz feta cheese, sliced
5ml/1 tsp chilli sauce
salt and ground black pepper
tomato salsa (see cook's tip), to serve

1 Place the quinoa in a pan with the water and bring to the boil over high heat, then reduce the heat and simmer, covered, for 20 minutes, until the water has been absorbed.

2 Slowly add the milk to the quinoa, stirring gently, then add the oil and the beaten eggs, still stirring.

3 Add the slices of cheese and the chilli sauce and season to taste. Cook for a further 2 minutes, stirring, then remove from the heat and serve hot, accompanied by a good tomato or onion salsa.

COOK'S TIP

For the tomato salsa, combine chopped tomatoes with finely sliced spring onions (scallions), chopped chilli, lime juice, salt and oil. This dish is a good accompaniment to grilled steak, if the meal is not vegetarian, but because of quinoa's high protein content it makes a meal in itself.

When the Spanish conquerors came to America they were looking for gold and silver, land and power. Today the minerals are depleted, but potato, corn, cassava, lucuma, quinoa and other plants remain. In Inca times quinoa was considered to be sacred, and the emperor would sow the first seeds of the season. It is important to wash the quinoa several times before using it, to remove any traces of saponine.

Squash, Potato and Corn Stew Locro de zapallo

Serves 6

75ml/5 tbsp vegetable oil
1 small onion, finely chopped
2 garlic cloves, finely sliced or chopped
1 medium tomato, chopped
1 butternut squash, weighing approximately 1kg/2¼lb, peeled and cut into 2.5cm/1in chunks
3 corn on the cob, cut into 2.5cm/1in chunks
1 kg/2¼lb white potatoes, peeled and quartered
500ml/17fl oz/2 cups water
100g/3¾oz feta cheese
salt
boiled white rice, to serve

A locro is a stew from the south of Peru. There is a very large yellow squash in Peru, called zapallo, which is soft and buttery and is used in many recipes. Butternut squash has been substituted here, and gives a delicious nutty flavour.

1 Heat the oil in a large pan over medium heat and fry the onion and garlic for 10 minutes, until the onion is browned. Add the tomato, and cook for another 5 minutes.

2 Add the pieces of squash, corn on the cob and potatoes to the pan and pour in the water. Season with salt, bring to the boil and cook over medium heat for 20 minutes, covered, until the potatoes are tender.

3 Remove the pan from the heat and crumble the cheese over the vegetables. Serve immediately, accompanied by boiled white rice.

COOK'S TIP

To prepare the butternut squash it is best to peel it first. The skin is thin, and comes off easily with a vegetable peeler. When peeled, remove the top and bottom and chop it in half lengthways, remove the seeds and filaments and cut into chunks.

Dried Peas Alverjitas secas

Serves 4

250g/9oz/1¼ cups dried peas, soaked for 8 hours, and drained
1.5 litres/2½ pints/6¼ cups water
75ml/5 tbsp olive oil
1 medium onion, finely diced
1 small tomato, chopped
salt
boiled white rice and onion salsa (see p18), to serve

Dried beans, peas and lentils are part of the staple diet all over America. Many Peruvian dishes are enriched by the addition of ingredients such as onions fried in oil, and all beans are very good treated in this way, whichever variety you use – the only difference will be in the cooking times. This dish can be a meal in itself, or accompany any meat course.

1 Place the peas in a large pan with the water and bring to the boil, then reduce the heat and simmer, covered, for 1 hour, until soft. Stir from time to time to prevent them sticking. If they start to dry out, add a little extra boiling water from the kettle, but not too much at a time.

2 Heat the oil in a frying pan and gently fry the onion for about 10 minutes, until browned. Add the tomato and cook for a further 5 minutes.

3 Pour the onion and tomato mixture, together with all the oil, over the peas and stir it in. Season to taste and leave for 15 minutes for the flavours to infuse before serving with rice and onion salsa.

VARIATION

To make a richer dish, try adding some chopped smoked bacon or sausage for extra flavour. Peruvians often add a piece of pork skin to the pot while boiling dried beans to make them softer.

Sweet Potato Purée Pure de camotes

Serves 8

1kg/2¼lb yellow sweet potatoes, preferably South American
15ml/1 tbsp butter
75ml/5 tbsp caster (superfine) sugar
juice of 1 orange

The sweet potato probably originated in Central America. It is much used in Peru, where it is usually served boiled with savoury dishes such as cebiche or escabeche, or baked for a sweeter result. Fried sweet potato is indispensable for a good chicharrones sandwich, and its sweet flavour is also delicious in desserts. This purée is an excellent accompaniment for roasted meats such as pork or turkey.

1 Put the sweet potatoes in a large pan with enough water to cover and boil them in their skins for 30 minutes, covered, until tender. Drain and peel them as soon as they are cool enough to handle.

2 Mash the peeled sweet potatoes and return them to the pan. Stir in the butter and sugar and cook gently for about 8 minutes, stirring constantly to avoid the mixture sticking.

3 Off the heat, stir the orange juice into the purée and serve immediately, topped with extra butter, if you wish.

VARIATION

For an extra-sweet version of this recipe, pour the purée into an ovenproof dish and dot the top with marshmallows. Bake for 20–30 minutes in a moderate oven until the purée is heated through and the marshmallows are melting and golden.

Purple Corn Pudding Mazamorra morada

Serves 6

1 sachet purple corn powder
1 apple, roughly chopped
1 cinnamon stick
3 cloves
1 small piece (2cm/¾in) dried orange peel
1½ litres/2½ pints/6¼ cups water
50g/2oz prunes
50g/2oz dried apricots
50g/2oz dried peaches
50g/2oz dried pears
90ml/6 tbsp sugar
45ml/3 tbsp potato flour (starch)
ground cinnamon, for dusting

This confection of corn and dried fruits, thickened with sweet potato starch, is quintessentially Peruvian. Traditionally fed to children to give them energy, there are many variations, using ingredients such as squash, flour and molasses, quinoa or tapioca. All are sweet, healthy and gentle on the stomach.

1 Place the sachet of corn powder in a large pan with the apple, cinnamon stick, cloves and orange peel. Stir in the water and bring to the boil. Simmer for 30 minutes over medium heat.

2 Strain the mixture and return the liquid to the pan. Add the dried fruits and simmer for a further 30 minutes, then stir in the sugar.

3 Blend the potato flour with 100ml/3½fl oz/scant ½ cup water and add it to the pan, stir for 5 minutes until the mixture thickens, then remove from the heat.

4 Pour into a serving bowl, or into individual bowls (distributing the fruit evenly). Dust with cinnamon and leave to cool before serving.

Spiced Rice Pudding Arroz zambito

Serves 6

250g/9oz/1¼ cups white rice
1 litre/1¾ pints/4 cups water
3 cinnamon sticks
3 cloves
250g/9oz/1¼ cups soft dark brown sugar
45ml/3 tbsp desiccated (dry unsweetened shredded) coconut
100g/3¾oz/⅔ cup raisins
45ml/3 tbsp chopped walnuts
350ml/12fl oz evaporated milk
ground cinnamon, to dust

In a culture in which rice is eaten every day it would be impossible not to have some desserts made with it, and Peru has several favourites. Milk pudding made with rice is a popular dish in many other countries, but the spices, fruits and dark brown sugar in this Peruvian version make it uniquely delicious.

1 Wash the rice. Put the water in a large heavy pan with the cinnamon sticks, cloves and sugar and bring to the boil.

2 Add the rice and the coconut. Cook over a medium-high heat, stirring often, for 20–25 minutes or until the rice is cooked.

3 Add the raisins, walnuts and evaporated milk, and simmer for 10 minutes, stirring from time to time.

4 Spoon into small dishes, and leave to cool. Dust with cinnamon before serving. Use the cooked cinnamon sticks as a garnish, if you like.

Sigh of a Lima Woman
Suspiro de Limeña

Serves 6

350ml/12fl oz/1¼ cups sweetened condensed milk
350ml/12fl oz/1½ cups evaporated milk
5 egg yolks
5ml/1 tsp vanilla extract
250g/9oz/1¼ cups caster (superfine) sugar
250ml/8fl oz white port or white vermouth
3 egg whites
ground cinnamon, to dust

1 To make the dulce de leche, on which this recipe is based, mix the condensed and evaporated milks together in a pan.

2 Bring slowly to the boil and then cook over medium heat for 40 minutes, stirring constantly to prevent burning, until reduced and thick. The colour should have changed from cream to a light toffee colour. Remove from the heat and leave to cool a little.

3 When the dulce de leche has cooled slightly, but is still warm, add the egg yolks and vanilla to the mixture and stir thoroughly. Pour into individual serving dishes and leave to cool.

4 To make the topping, combine the sugar with the port or vermouth in a small pan. Heat gently, stirring, until the sugar has dissolved, then bring to the boil and cook the syrup over a high heat for 7 minutes.

5 Meanwhile, whisk the egg whites until they form stiff peaks. Still whisking, pour the hot syrup into the whites and continue to whisk until the meringue is cool and thick.

6 Pile the meringue on top of the caramel mixture, dust with cinnamon and serve.

The women of Lima have always been famed for their wit and beauty, and the story goes that after tasting this dessert a 19th-century poet commented, "It is like the sigh of a lady from Lima." There was no more to say: the sweet had its name. The basis of this pudding is dulce de leche, the sweet fudge sauce made from reduced condensed milk, which is adored by all South Americans.

COOK'S TIP

Suspiro de Limeña is extremely rich, so it's best served in small portions.

Chicken Neck Pastries Guarguero

Makes 16

- 30ml/2 tbsp self-raising (self-rising) flour, plus extra for dusting
- 5ml/1 tsp baking powder
- 2 egg yolks
- 50g/2oz/¼ cup margarine
- 30ml/2 tbsp pisco or grappa
- vegetable oil, for frying
- 1 egg white, lightly beaten
- 400g/14oz can dulce de leche (see page 58) or sweetened condensed milk
- 45ml/3 tbsp icing (confectioners') sugar for dusting

1 Sift the flour and baking powder into a bowl, make a well in the centre and add the egg yolks and margarine.

2 Mix the flour, egg and margarine together, gradually adding the pisco or grappa. Knead the dough until smooth, then cover and leave to rest for 1 hour.

3 Dust the work surface with flour and roll the dough out very thinly (about 2mm/1/12in). Cut the dough into small triangles about 7.5cm/3in across.

4 Heat the oil in a frying pan. When it is hot, start rolling up the triangles into cylinders, beginning at a long side and securing the apex with a little egg white. Work quickly, and drop each cylinder into the pan as soon as it is formed so that it keeps its shape.

5 Fry the pastries over a medium heat for about 3 minutes, turning them carefully, until they are crisp and golden.

6 As the pastries are done, remove them from the pan with a slotted spoon and drain on kitchen paper. Leave to cool completely.

7 Fill the pastries with dulce de leche, spooning or piping it from both ends, and dust them with sifted icing sugar before serving. If not serving immediately, keep in an airtight container, then fill and dust just before serving.

Many Peruvian sweets have amusing or charming names that describe their appearance, such as 'little handkerchiefs' and 'flying saucers', and these delicious caramel-filled fried pastries are called 'chicken necks'. They are sold in bakeries and at street stalls. Crisp and light, they can be served as a dessert or as a snack with a cup of tea or coffee.

Wedding Biscuits Empanaditas de boda

Makes 15

250g/9oz/2¼ cups self-raising (self-rising) flour
10ml/2 tsp baking powder
250g/9oz/1¼ cups caster (superfine) sugar
250g/9oz/generous 1 cup lard
30ml/2 tbsp water
1 egg yolk
45ml/3 tbsp milk
50g/2oz/¼ cup toasted sesame seeds

1 Preheat the oven to 200°C/400°F/Gas 6 and grease a large baking sheet.

2 Sift the flour with the baking powder and stir in the sugar. Make a well in the centre and add the lard, cut into small pieces, and the water. Gradually rub the lard and water in to the dry ingredients, adding a little more water if needed, and knead the mixture for about 10 minutes to form a smooth dough.

3 Form the dough into a roll about 7.5cm/3in in diameter and cut it into 1cm/½in slices.

4 Lay the slices on the baking sheet, spacing them well.

5 Beat the egg yolk lightly with the milk and brush the top of each biscuit with the mixture. Sprinkle with the sesame seeds and bake for 20 minutes, until they are golden brown. Leave them on the baking sheet to cool.

In some towns in the North Central region these biscuits are sold at local festivals. They are known as 'wedding biscuits' because they are most often made for such celebrations, but street vendors also sell them, freshly made, warm and delicious.

Nutritional notes

Fried Pork with Onion Salsa: Energy 510kcal/2107kJ; Protein 19.4g; Carbohydrate 2g, of which sugars 1.4g; Fat 47.2g, of which saturates 16.7g; Cholesterol 90mg; Calcium 16mg; Fibre 0.4g; Sodium 92mg.
Marinated Fish: Energy 145kcal/612kJ; Protein 18.7g; Carbohydrate 9.3g, of which sugars 8.1g; Fat 4g, of which saturates 0.7g; Cholesterol 85mg; Calcium 67mg; Fibre 1.7g; Sodium 126mg.
Potatoes in Peanut Sauce: Energy 432kcal/1799kJ; Protein 15.8g; Carbohydrate 23.1g, of which sugars 7.2g; Fat 31.4g, of which saturates 5.2g; Cholesterol 95mg; Calcium 56mg; Fibre 4.1g; Sodium 102mg.
Broad Bean and Fresh Cheese Salad: Energy 293kcal/1225kJ; Protein 12.6g; Carbohydrate 24.6g, of which sugars 4.6g; Fat 16.7g, of which saturates 6.5g; Cholesterol 26mg; Calcium 175mg; Fibre 5g; Sodium 620mg.
Peruvian Beef Pies: Energy 223kcal/930kJ; Protein 8g; Carbohydrate 15.3g, of which sugars 0.9g; Fat 14.9g, of which saturates 4.8g; Cholesterol 27mg; Calcium 26mg; Fibre 0.8g; Sodium 61mg.
Corn Parcels: Energy 429kcal/1790kJ; Protein 9.9g; Carbohydrate 45.8g, of which sugars 9.3g; Fat 23.4g, of which saturates 7.5g; Cholesterol 67mg; Calcium 22mg; Fibre 2.3g; Sodium 232mg.
Butter Bean Soup: Energy 305kcal/1280kJ; Protein 14.9g; Carbohydrate 31.9g, of which sugars 4.5g; Fat 14.1g, of which saturates 3.7g; Cholesterol 13mg; Calcium 187mg; Fibre 7.4g; Sodium 241mg.
Crayfish Soup: Energy 466kcal/1956kJ; Protein 38.2g; Carbohydrate 41.5g, of which sugars 5.9g; Fat 17.1g, of which saturates 2.9g; Cholesterol 365mg; Calcium 119mg; Fibre 4.4g; Sodium 426mg.
Beef Hotpot: Energy 709kcal/2995kJ; Protein 61.1g; Carbohydrate 81.6g, of which sugars 34.3g; Fat 17.7g, of which saturates 6.7g; Cholesterol 135mg; Calcium 217mg; Fibre 13g; Sodium 433mg.
Corn Purée with Fried Fish: Energy 508kcal/2122kJ; Protein 31.7g; Carbohydrate 35.3g, of which sugars 10.6g; Fat 27.5g, of which saturates 3g; Cholesterol 69mg; Calcium 57mg; Fibre 2.4g; Sodium 393mg.
Dry Fish Stew with Coriander: Energy 302kcal/1257kJ; Protein 31.5g; Carbohydrate 9.6g, of which sugars 5.4g; Fat 14.9g, of which saturates 1.6g; Cholesterol 69mg; Calcium 63mg; Fibre 3.5g; Sodium 183mg.
Fried Seafood Platter: Energy 747kcal/3141kJ; Protein 41.8g; Carbohydrate 86.7g, of which sugars 7.4g; Fat 28.2g, of which saturates 3.3g; Cholesterol 153mg; Calcium 114mg; Fibre 3.7g; Sodium 607mg.
Beef Stew with Carrots and Potatoes: Energy 582kcal/2426kJ; Protein 37.3g; Carbohydrate 43.5g, of which sugars 16.7g; Fat 30g, of which saturates 6.9g; Cholesterol 73mg; Calcium 77mg; Fibre 8g; Sodium 261mg.
Lamb Stew with Boiled Cassava: Energy 662kcal/2771kJ; Protein 34.2g; Carbohydrate 62.1g, of which sugars 16.1g; Fat 32.6g, of which saturates 8.7g; Cholesterol 95mg; Calcium 113mg; Fibre 9.2g; Sodium 180mg.
Rabbit in Peanut Sauce: Energy 559kcal/2324kJ; Protein 35.2g; Carbohydrate 9g, of which sugars 5g; Fat 38.3g, of which saturates 6.9g; Cholesterol 71mg; Calcium 63mg; Fibre 3.4g; Sodium 72mg.
Turkey and Corn Stew: Energy 472kcal/1980kJ; Protein 34g; Carbohydrate 42g, of which sugars 15.9g; Fat 19.8g, of which saturates 2.4g; Cholesterol 61mg; Calcium 24mg; Fibre 2.5g; Sodium 461mg.
Duck with Rice: Energy 981kcal/4083kJ; Protein 33.2g; Carbohydrate 116.9g, of which sugars 10.5g; Fat 39.1g, of which saturates 7.9g; Cholesterol 75mg; Calcium 72mg; Fibre 4.6g; Sodium 122mg.
Cassava Stuffed with Cheese: Energy 548kcal/2299kJ; Protein 14.3g; Carbohydrate 66.2g, of which sugars 14.5g; Fat 26.7g, of which saturates 7.6g; Cholesterol 58mg; Calcium 345mg; Fibre 6.5g; Sodium 452mg.
Quinoa Stew: Energy 501kcal/2082kJ; Protein 21.3g; Carbohydrate 39.5g, of which sugars 7.4g; Fat 29.6g, of which saturates 12.1g; Cholesterol 149mg; Calcium 414mg; Fibre 0g; Sodium 1007mg.
Squash, Potato and Corn Stew: Energy 329kcal/1382kJ; Protein 8.3g; Carbohydrate 45.2g, of which sugars 11g; Fat 14g, of which saturates 3.7g; Cholesterol 12mg; Calcium 124mg; Fibre 4.3g; Sodium 395mg.
Dried Peas: Energy 331kcal/1388kJ; Protein 15.2g; Carbohydrate 36.9g, of which sugars 2.9g; Fat 14.6g, of which saturates 2.1g; Cholesterol 0mg; Calcium 37mg; Fibre 3.4g; Sodium 25mg.
Sweet Potato Purée: Energy 162kcal/689kJ; Protein 1.6g; Carbohydrate 37g, of which sugars 17.5g; Fat 1.9g, of which saturates 1.1g; Cholesterol 4mg; Calcium 36mg; Fibre 3g; Sodium 65mg.
Purple Corn Pudding: Energy 122kcal/518kJ; Protein 1.8g; Carbohydrate 29.4g, of which sugars 23.4g; Fat 0.3g, of which saturates 0g; Cholesterol 0mg; Calcium 29mg; Fibre 2.4g; Sodium 6mg.
Spiced Rice Pudding: Energy 518kcal/2181kJ; Protein 9.7g; Carbohydrate 95.1g, of which sugars 61.8g; Fat 12.5g, of which saturates 5.9g; Cholesterol 10mg; Calcium 198mg; Fibre 1.6g; Sodium 82mg.
Sigh of a Lima Woman: Energy 308kcal/1292kJ; Protein 11.9g; Carbohydrate 38.4g, of which sugars 38.4g; Fat 12.9g, of which saturates 6.4g; Cholesterol 199mg; Calcium 340mg; Fibre 0g; Sodium 156mg.
Chicken Neck Pastries: Energy 169kcal/708kJ; Protein 2.9g; Carbohydrate 18.3g, of which sugars 16.8g; Fat 9.5g, of which saturates 2.4g; Cholesterol 34mg; Calcium 80mg; Fibre 0.1g; Sodium 40mg.
Wedding Biscuits: Energy 295kcal/1230kJ; Protein 2.5g; Carbohydrate 30.2g, of which sugars 17.8g; Fat 19.1g, of which saturates 7.2g; Cholesterol 29mg; Calcium 95mg; Fibre 0.8g; Sodium 64mg.

Index